Take a Look!
Modern Media Literacy

What's the Purpose?

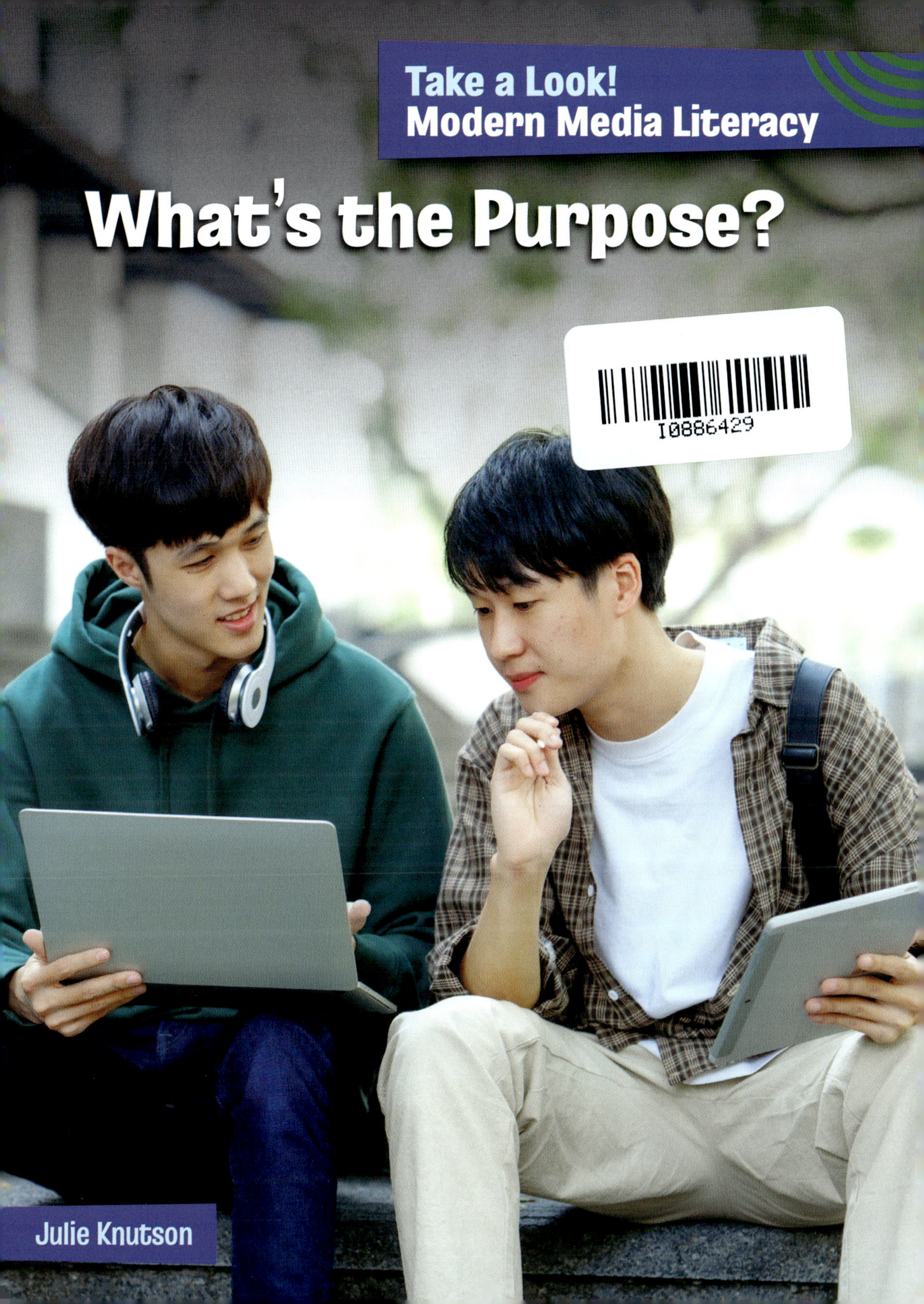

Julie Knutson

Cherry Lake Press

Published in the United States of America by Cherry Lake Publishing Group
Ann Arbor, Michigan
www.cherrylakepublishing.com

Reading Adviser: Beth Walker Gambro, MS, Ed., Reading Consultant, Yorkville, IL
Content Adviser: Kristin Fontichiaro, Clinical Professor, University of Michigan School of Information

Photo Credits: © NTshutterth/Shutterstock, cover, title page; © Jacob Lund/Shutterstock, 5; © Oleksii Didok/Shutterstock, 6; © HJBC/Shutterstock, 7; © Ground Picture/Shutterstock, 8; © Pixel-Shot/Shutterstock, 9; © G-Stock Studio/Shutterstock, 10; © silverkblackstock/Shutterstock, 11; © Phoenixns/Shutterstock, 12; © Dean Drobot/Shutterstock, 13; © Arlette Lopez/Shutterstock, 15, 17, 18; © Featureflash/Dreamstime.com, 19; © Arlette Lopez/Shutterstock, 20, 21, 22; © l i g h t p o e t/Shutterstock, 23; © DC Studio/Shutterstock, 25; © Alberto Menendez Cervero/Shutterstock, 26; © Alina Rosanova/Shutterstock, 28; © alvarog1970/Shutterstock, 30; © CGN089/Shutterstock, 31

Cherry Lake Press is an imprint of Cherry Lake Publishing Group.

Library of Congress Cataloging-in-Publication Data

Names: Knutson, Julie, author.
Title: What's the purpose? / written by Julie Knutson.
Description: Ann Arbor, Michigan : Cherry Lake Publishing, 2025. | Series: Take a look! modern media literacy | Audience: Grades 4-6 | Summary: "Part of our Take a Look! Modern Media Literacy series, What's the Point? examines the author's purpose always present in media, how to spot it, and how to use it intentionally to inform, persuade, and entertain. Series closely aligned with standards from the American Association of School Librarians and the Journalism Education Association. This series gives readers a crash course in basic media literacy skills: understanding audience, perspective, persuasive appeals, author's purpose, tracing sources, and creating media content"—Provided by publisher.
Identifiers: LCCN 2024035960 | ISBN 9781668956359 (hardcover) | ISBN 9781668957202 (paperback) | ISBN 9781668958070 (ebook) | ISBN 9781668958940 (pdf)
Subjects: LCSH: Media literacy—Juvenile literature. | Exposition (Rhetoric)—Juvenile literature. | Persuasion (Rhetoric) in mass media—Juvenile literature. | Mass media—Authorship—Juvenile literature.
Classification: LCC P96.M4 K586 2025 | DDC 302.23—dc23/eng/20240828
LC record available at https://lccn.loc.gov/2024035960

Cherry Lake Press would like to acknowledge the work of the Partnership for 21st Century Learning, a Network of Battelle for Kids. Please visit Battelle for Kids online for more information.

Printed in the United States of America

Note from publisher: Websites change regularly, and their future contents are outside of our control. Supervise children when conducting any recommended online searches for extended learning opportunities.

Julie Knutson (she/her) is an author and educator who lives and works in Philadelphia, PA. She's no stranger to navigating media in our modern world, and she teaches her students to do the same. Whether working with students to craft interview questions or debating designs for a classroom magazine, she also loves guiding middle schoolers through the media-making process.

CONTENTS

CHAPTER 1

Take a Look! The Big Picture

Chances are you're online . . . a lot. In fact, studies show that kids from 8–12 spend an average of 8 hours and 39 minutes a day on screens. Teens? Seven hours and 22 minutes a day. You probably already know how kids and teens spend that time—you're one of them after all. They watch TV and videos. They play games. They scroll social media. Sound familiar?

At least 43 percent of kids' and teens' time awake is spent this way. They are viewing hundreds, thousands, and even millions of pieces of **media** each year. But all content is not created equal.

How can you find out which information you can rely on? How can you decide which is worth sharing? One of the most important questions to ask is *What is the creator's purpose?* What does that mean? Let's take a look and find out.

Sharing ideas with others got much easier with the internet. Now media can be shared at about two-thirds the speed of light!

“About Me” or “About Us” pages on websites can be helpful places to go to find out more about why the creator may have created their media.

Consider a recipe for brownies you see shared. How can you tell if this recipe is worth a try? The recipe is on a blog. The “About Me” page says the author was a professional pastry chef for 20 years. He loves sharing his passion for baking. You look at some of his other blog posts. There are ads on the sides of each page.

Print or digital billboard ads usually have one of the following purposes: to convince you to do or buy something, to vote for someone or something, or to spread knowledge or opinions.

Sponsored content takes many forms. It could be an unboxing video. It could be an ad in a magazine designed to look like part of an article. It could be a link that shows up at the top of your search engine results.

The author does have some posts marked as “sponsored content.” This is when he’s partnering with a company to promote their product. The brownie recipe breakdown? Not labeled as sponsored content. No specific brands are even mentioned. The author shares tips and tricks to get the recipe just right. He breaks down each step. He includes pictures to help you learn. This looks like a reliable recipe.

Learning why that media’s creator made it is important. The blog post about the brownie recipe? The author wanted to inform. He wanted to share his passion for baking. Figuring this out helped you decide that this media held quality content. The more you learn about being media savvy, the more confident you can be with media online and offline!

Unpacking a Creator's Purpose

Creators share work with an **audience** for three main reasons—to inform, persuade, and entertain. But sometimes there's more below the surface. Sometimes creators also have a **motivation** behind what they make. Maybe they make a YouTube video to persuade you to buy a sponsored product. Their motivation might be to get paid by their sponsor. Perhaps the creator makes an informative Instagram reel about dog training. Their motivation may be to gain more followers and clients for their dog training business. Some creators

THINK & ENGAGE

Why do you think THIS book was written? Do you think its purpose is to inform, persuade, or entertain?

The motivation behind a piece of media may not be what it seems at first. You may have to dig a bit deeper to figure it out.

are motivated by the possibility of fame. They want to be well-known! It's good to be able to see not only the creator's purpose but the motivation behind it too.

A creator may make media with the purpose to inform. Informational media ranges from how-to videos to cookbooks. Its goal is to teach about a topic. Persuasive media exists to convince a person of something.

IS THERE SUCH A THING AS "MULTI-PURPOSE MEDIA"?

Can media have more than one purpose? Absolutely!

Think about Super Bowl commercials. Whether marketing cars or candy, shoes, or soda, the aim of these ads is to sell. Advertisers create them to persuade people to buy their products.

But there's more to it than that. Successful ads inform viewers about what they're selling. They also entertain, making viewers laugh, cry, or even sing along. They make the audience want to be a part of that product's story. And when people are still thinking and talking about the ad afterward? Bonus! It helps promote the product even more.

Companies spend millions of dollars developing ads that strike all these chords.

A persuasive media creator makes a claim and supports it with evidence and **reasoning**. A claim is something the creator wants people to believe. Advertisements, or ads, are always meant to be persuasive. They work to convince people to buy, vote for, or believe something. Finally, some media is intended to entertain. Comedy shows and cartoons, graphic novels, humorous podcasts . . . these are all produced with enjoyment in mind.

Maybe a video comes across your feed about an actor you like. Its creator is saying this actor doesn't care about their fans. The creator argues that fans should boycott the actor's movies! Wait a second—should you really do that? This video is trying to persuade you to stop watching certain movies. You learn that the creator is angry at the actor because the creator didn't get an interview with them. You know the actor does lots of fan appearances. You don't like or share the video because it is mean-spirited and not persuasive.

Why ask, "What is the purpose of this media?" It's important to be able to identify a creator's purpose. It's important to think about the motivation behind it. Why did they make their media? If it doesn't align with what you need, want, or value, you can move on.

CHAPTER 2

Break It Down! How People Get Their Point Across

How can you spot a creator's purpose? Let's learn!

Meet expert Rubik's Cube solver Paz!

Paz loves watching Rubik's cube videos. She follows lots of creators. She wants to share some videos with her cousins to help them learn how to solve Rubik's cubes, too. Then they can all cube together during summer break!

She's been learning about creator's purpose in school. Her teacher told her this could help her decide if she wants to continue engaging with media and then find the media she needs. Let's see how she uses what she knows to sort through these videos.

Paz feels like this is a great time to practice spotting creator's purpose!

Persuade

Paz finds her first video about Rubik's Cubes. This creator starts off with, "Thanks for joining me for this Rubik's Master demo!" The creator starts a timer. He solves the Rubik's Master. He starts talking about how a 4x4 cube is even more fun than a classic 3x3 cube. He ends the video with, "Use code rubiksmaster20 for 20 percent off! And don't forget to click like, follow, and subscribe!" This creator didn't show *how* to solve a Rubik's Cube. And it wasn't even a classic Rubik's Cube. Paz reads the description under the video. She sees "#RubiksPartner." She realizes this video is an ad. Clearly, this creator's purpose was to persuade. He was trying to convince her to buy the 4x4 Rubik's Cube. Not what she was looking for. She moves on to another video.

THINK & INQUIRE

Think about the media you use the most. Do you watch YouTube videos? TikToks? Reels? Do you read articles? Watch shows? Listen to podcasts? The next time you watch or listen to media, try to spot its purpose. Does the creator want to inform, persuade, or entertain?

If you can start to identify purpose in media, you can make decisions like Paz. If media doesn't fit your wants or needs, you can move on.

Paz knows the creators of these videos have different motivations behind why they made them. She thinks through possibilities as she watches.

Entertain

This video seems like more of a fit. The creator starts off with, "Welcome, Cubies! Let's have some fun!" 3x3 cube? Check. No #ad, #sponsored content, #partner mentions? Check. But something still doesn't quite feel right. Paz continues watching. The creator starts shifting the sides of the cube. But wait! The creator tosses the cube in the air, catches it on the back of one arm, and lets it roll over her shoulders to her other hand. She then flips it back and catches it in front of her. She switches around the sides of the cube two more times. Then she tosses it in the air, does a front flip, and catches it again. Whoa! This is so cool! Paz smiles. She realizes the purpose of this video is to entertain. But this is not what Paz needs for her cousins. She keeps looking.

Paz already has a good feeling about this last video. She thinks it may have a purpose that matches what she's looking for!

Inform

Paz finds another video. The creator captures the audience's attention right from the start. He says, "Think it's impossible to solve a Rubik's Cube? Think again!" The creator continues to explain his main idea—that viewers can learn how to solve a Rubik's Cube. He breaks down how to solve the cube step-by-step. He goes over complicated steps twice. He shows the steps from different angles. He then holds up the finished Rubik's Cube in victory! He closes with, "There you have it. Reach out with questions. And let me know how it goes down in the comments section!" It was a 3x3 cube.

FILMMAKING WITH A PURPOSE: ZURIEL ODUWOLE

How are young people using media with the purpose to inform and persuade in the real world? Zuriel Oduwole has used media to advocate for others since she was 9 years old.

For more than 10 years, Zuriel has informed people about educational issues across the globe. She's used filmmaking to advocate for **gender equality**. Today, she runs workshops for young people. Why? In her words, she wants to "teach people the skills to tell their own stories."

She's met with more than 35 presidents and **prime ministers**. She's traveled to more than 20 countries to encourage students to finish their studies. She is a filmmaker and education activist with a purpose.

For Zuriel, making films is purposeful. It allows her to tell positive stories and untold histories. Through movies, she can also reach new audiences. She can bring other people's attention to issues like quality education. Through movies, she can make a change.

Building confidence in choosing media takes time. You can practice your purpose-spotting skills with any media you see or hear.

No #ad, #sponsoredcontent, or #partner is mentioned beneath the video. And the creator did a great job teaching the steps! Nothing too fancy. The purpose of this video is definitely to inform. Paz thinks this video will be great for her cousins.

Her final step? Share it with her cousins! They're excited to get it. After three views, they solve the cube. Success!

Paz found what she needed. She was able to sort through videos using her knowledge of creator's purpose. The first creator wanted to sell Paz something. His purpose? To persuade. The second creator wanted to show off some cool Rubik's tricks. Purpose? To entertain. The final video? A step-by-step informative video on how to solve a Rubik's Cube. Paz was glad she knew how to find what she was looking for!

GROW & ENGAGE

Use the knowledge you've gained about creator's purpose. Think through your own media goals. Do you need media for a project at school? Media to teach a friend something? Media to win someone over to your viewpoint? Search for the media you need. Do you want media that entertains? Informs? Persuades?

CHAPTER 3

Show What You Know! Find the Purpose

When you view media—whether a video, article, podcast, or anything else—identify the creator's purpose. Does that creator want to inform others about a topic? Persuade people? Entertain an audience? Identify the reason! You can use some tried-and-true methods to do this. Tapping into these methods makes you a savvier consumer.

Let's cover some tips that will help you get started on your own.

It can be helpful to write down your thoughts about the media you hear or see. It can help you reflect. It can help you decide if it's right for you.

You can also compare media on the same topic. Does it all seem to have the same purpose? Different purposes?

First, ask these questions:

- Is it providing information?
- Is it asking the audience to do or believe something?
- Is it using humor, music, or other elements?

Then, check for clues in these places:

- A creator's "About Me" page
- A note or tag that marks it "Sponsored," "Promoted," or an "Ad"
- A bibliography or works cited
- Reviews or comments from other audience members

CREATE & EXPLORE

The next time you create media with a specific purpose, get audience feedback. Did they think the media fulfilled its purpose? Reflect on what they say. Go through a redesign of your media with their feedback in mind.

Sometimes it's helpful to ask for other people's opinions on media. Do they see the same purpose? Can they help you decide if you want to support it?

Once you've answered these questions about the media, you can make an informed decision! Do you want to support the creator's purpose? If so, like and share! If not, move on! Remember that a creator's purposes often overlap. A kids' TV show? It could be entertaining and informative. And a speech's primary purpose might be to persuade, but it can also be informational and entertaining.

THE PURPOSE BEHIND DEEPFAKES

Maybe you've heard of **deepfakes**. Deepfakes are images or videos of people that have been changed using artificial intelligence (AI). That picture of the pope wearing a Balenciaga jacket? Deepfake. Those Tom Cruise TikToks where he's saying or doing strange things? Deepfakes.

How can you tell if a video or image is a deepfake? Does the skin look too smooth? Does the skin tone of the face match the skin tone of the rest of the body? If it's a video, do the lips match the words the person is saying? Do the teeth look weird? Another thing you can look at is the lighting. Do the shadows line up with the light source? Does the background look real?

Also, consider the context! If you see a picture of the pope wearing a designer jacket, stop to think about it. Is this something the pope would normally do? Is it realistic?

A deepfake may have been made for entertainment. The creator may have wanted to make people laugh. But it's important to be able to question the purpose. Maybe you spot a deepfake that seems to have been made to spread false information. You can choose not to share it with others. You can choose not to look at or listen to it.

Do More!

Extension Activity

Aaaaand . . . the theme is HOBBIES! The range of choices is vast. Making music, skateboarding, cooking, and horseback riding are just a few examples.

Choose your favorite hobby. Your challenge is to create a piece of media based on it.

Your first step? Define your purpose. Do you want to convince people your hobby is the best? Do you want to show off your hobby to entertain people? Do you want to teach viewers how to do your hobby on their own?

Next? Get working on your media! Apply the tips and tricks from this book. No matter the purpose, you need to do your research. It also helps to test out rough drafts on an audience. Then you know how you need to revise.

Remember that the purpose of media is to share it. Send it to family and friends. Invite teachers and classmates to view it. YOU have ideas worth sharing . . . pass them on!

Learn More

Books

Down, Susan Brophy. *Power and Persuasion in Media and Advertising.* New York, NY: Crabtree, 2018.

Loewen, Nancy. *Writing Powerful Persuasive Pieces.* Minneapolis, MN: Lerner, 2016.

Vander Hook, Sue. *Writing Intriguing Informational Pieces.* Minneapolis, MN: Lerner, 2016.

On the Web

Search these online sources with an adult:

McGraw Hill PreK-12—Author's Purpose Video | YouTube

PBS—Author's Purpose and Viewpoint

The New Times Rwanda—Zuriel Oduwole: 'World's most powerful girl' message to Rwandan girls video | YouTube

Glossary

audience (AW-dee-uhns) a person or group who hears or sees something

bibliography (BIB-lee-ah-gruh-fee) a list of sources referenced for the creation of a piece of media

deepfakes (DEEP-fayks) photos or images that have been changed, using AI, to make the people in them appear to be different people

gender equality (JEN-duhr ih-KWAH-luh-tee) equal treatment and opportunity for people of all genders

media (MEE-dee-uh) the means of communicating information to large numbers of people, including television, newspapers, magazines, and radio

motivation (moh-tuh-VAY-shuhn) a reason for doing something

prime ministers (PRIYM MIH-nuh-stuhrz) elected or appointed leaders of some countries

reasoning (REE-zuhn-ing) using logic to form an idea or opinion about something

Index